40 Days
to Your Transformed You

Daily Words for Personal Development Devotional

By

Yolanda V Wiggins

Published by Unlimited Life
Gotha, FL 34734
Copyright © 2024 by Yolanda V Wiggins

40 Days
to Your Transformed You

Daily Words for Personal Development Devotional

Table of Contents

Introduction

Welcome to "40 Days to a Transformed You." In the intricate tapestry of sacred scripture, the number "40" stands out as a symbol charged with deep significance—a symbol representing new life, flourishing growth, and transformative change. It represents a transition from one great task to another, a period of preparation, self-examination, and ultimately, fulfillment.

In the pages that follow, we embark on a 40-day journey inspired by the biblical richness of the number 40. Just as the Great Flood brought forth a new era of life and the Manna sustained the Israelites for 40 years, so too will these 40 days be a catalyst for personal growth, renewal, and spiritual nourishment.

Consider the Scriptural narrative: Moses receiving the Law atop Mount Sinai after 40 days, the Israelites' wandering in the desert, and Jesus fasting for 40 days to prepare for His public ministry. Each instance bears witness to the transformative power encapsulated in the number 40—a number that signifies repentance, newness, and escape from the bondage of sin.

This journey mirrors the gestation period of new life, the seeking of indulgences, and the interval between Christmas and the Presentation, aligning with the scriptural undertones of fulfillment and redemption. Our daily words resonate with these qualities, guiding you through self-reflection, personal development, and the path to an unlimited life.

As you delve into each daily word, may you find echoes of the biblical significance of "40" in your own life—a call to repentance, a preparation for transformative tasks, and a journey towards personal fulfillment. May this expedition be your spiritual ascent, much like Moses ascending Mount Sinai or Jesus preparing for His ministry.

Instructions for
Maximum Impact

Daily Devotion: Set aside a dedicated time each day to engage with the daily word. Reflect on its significance in your life and consider how it aligns with the transformative themes of the number 40.

Journaling: Keep a journal to document your thoughts, insights, and personal experiences during this 40-day journey. Capture moments of clarity, resilience, gratitude, courage, and balance.

Affirmations: Repeat the provided affirmations daily. Let them serve as reminders of the transformative truths encapsulated in each word, fostering a positive mindset and guiding your actions.

Prayer: Accompany each daily word with a moment of prayer. Use the suggested prayers or personalize them to align with your spiritual journey. Seek guidance, strength, and a deeper connection with the divine.

Discussion: Engage in discussions with fellow readers or a support group. Share your reflections, experiences, and insights. The collective journey can enhance the impact of this transformative process.

Application: Integrate the lessons learned into your daily life. Apply the principles of repentance, newness, and growth as you navigate challenges, make decisions, and interact with others.

May this 40-day journey be a transformative experience, guiding you toward an unlimited life rooted in the timeless wisdom of sacred scripture.

INTRODUCTION TO WEEK 1

Foundations of Growth

Welcome to Week 1 of your transformative journey, "Foundations of Growth." This week, we embark on a meaningful exploration of words that lay the groundwork for your personal and spiritual development. The five pillars we'll focus on are Growth, Resilience, Gratitude, Courage, and Balance.

Growth:

At the very core of this week's reflections is the concept of Growth. Just as a tiny seed transforms into a magnificent tree, your journey is about evolving, learning, and becoming the best version of yourself. Embrace the endless possibilities that growth brings, and let each day be a step forward on this path of continuous development.

Resilience:

Resilience, our second foundation, teaches us the strength found in bouncing back from challenges. Life may present hurdles, but like a resilient plant after a storm, you have the capacity to overcome difficulties and emerge stronger. Discover the power of resilience as a key element in your journey toward unlimited growth.

Gratitude:

Expressing Gratitude is a transformative practice that enriches our lives. By acknowledging the blessings around us, big and small, we cultivate a spirit of thankfulness. Gratitude becomes the fertile soil in which our personal growth can take root, fostering a heart that appreciates the beauty of the journey.

Courage:

Courage, the fourth pillar, propels us beyond comfort zones and fear. It's the force that enables us to face challenges, pursue dreams, and stand firm in our beliefs. Embrace courage as a guiding light, empowering you to navigate the twists and turns of your growth journey with boldness and determination.

Balance:

Lastly, we explore the importance of Balance. Just as a tightrope walker maintains equilibrium, finding balance in various aspects of life is crucial. Strive for harmony between work and rest, ambition and contentment, recognizing that a balanced life is conducive to sustainable growth.

As we delve into these foundational words, may this week serve as a solid base for the magnificent transformation that lies ahead. Open your heart to Growth, cultivate Resilience, practice Gratitude, summon Courage, and seek the delicate dance of Balance. Let these foundations be the pillars supporting your journey toward an unlimited life. May each word become a stepping stone, guiding you towards a more profound understanding of your boundless potential. Enjoy this week of foundational growth and exploration!

Growth

> "But grow in the grace and knowledge of our Lord and Savior Jesus Christ. To him be the glory both now and to the day of eternity. Amen."
>
> *– 2 Peter 3:18*

"Growth" is a divine invitation to participate actively in the abundant life that God has planned for us. In the scriptures, we find numerous references to the importance of growth, both spiritually and personally. Just as a seed planted in fertile soil flourishes into a strong and fruitful tree, our lives, when rooted in faith and nurtured by God's wisdom, have the potential to grow into something beautiful and purposeful. Recognizing the transformative power of growth encourages us to align our hearts with the divine will, trusting in God's guidance as we navigate the journey of life.

The Bible reminds us in 2 Peter 3:18, "But grow in the grace and knowledge of our Lord and Savior Jesus Christ. To him be the glory both now and to the day of eternity." This verse underscores the significance of continuous growth in our spiritual journey. It encourages us not only to seek knowledge but also to deepen our relationship with Christ, allowing His grace to permeate every aspect of our lives. In understanding this, we realize that our growth is not a solitary endeavor; it is a co-creation with God, a partnership where we are called to grow in His grace and reflect His glory in our daily existence.

As we meditate on the word "Growth" today, let us express our gratitude for the opportunities provided by God for our spiritual and personal development. May we remain steadfast in our commitment to growing in love, compassion, and understanding. Let our lives be a testimony to the transformative power of God's grace, illustrating that through Him, we can continually evolve into the individuals He intended us to be. In the spirit of 1 Thessalonians 5:18, "Give thanks in all circumstances; for this is the will of God in Christ Jesus for you," let us approach each day with gratitude, acknowledging that every moment is an opportunity for growth.

Prayer:

Heavenly Father, we come before you with hearts open to growth and transformation. Guide us on this journey, grant us the wisdom to discern your will, and fill our spirits with the grace and knowledge of our Lord and Savior, Jesus Christ. As we seek growth in every aspect of our lives, may our efforts be aligned with your divine purpose. We surrender our plans to you, trusting that through your grace, we will continue to grow and bring glory to your name. Amen.

Affirmation:

"I am a vessel of God's grace and knowledge. Each day, I grow in wisdom, love, and understanding, reflecting the glory of my Lord and Savior, Jesus Christ. I embrace the divine plan for my growth, trusting that through Him, I am continually transformed into the person God created me to be."

Resilience

> "I can do all things through him who strengthens me."
>
> *– Philippians 4:13*

"Resilience" stands as a testament to our unwavering strength, a quality deeply rooted in our reliance on God's empowering grace. In moments of adversity, the scripture from Philippians 4:13 serves as a guiding light: "I can do all things through him who strengthens me." This verse reminds us that our resilience is not self-derived but is a manifestation of God's strengthening presence in our lives. With Him as our source of strength, we are empowered to face challenges with unwavering courage, knowing that His grace enables us to navigate the storms of life.

Philippians 4:13 calls us to acknowledge our dependence on Christ for inner fortitude. Our resilience is not a solitary endeavor but a shared journey with the One who strengthens us. In cultivating resilience, we tap into the divine reservoir of courage and endurance, understanding that, with God, we can overcome any obstacle. Embracing resilience as a spiritual virtue allows us to face trials with a steadfast spirit, secure in the knowledge that God's strength is made perfect in our moments of weakness.

Today, as we focus on the word "Resilience," let us draw inspiration from the biblical assurance that God's strength is our anchor in times of trouble. May our hearts be fortified with the unwavering belief that, through Christ, we can endure and triumph over life's challenges. As we encounter difficulties, let us echo the words of Philippians 4:13, affirming our reliance on the divine strength that sustains us. With gratitude in our hearts, we acknowledge that our resilience is a reflection of God's enduring love and empowerment.

Prayer:

Heavenly Father, in moments of challenge, we turn to you for the resilience that surpasses our own strength. Fill us with the assurance that, through Christ, we can overcome any obstacle. Grant us the courage to face adversity with unwavering faith, knowing that your strength empowers us. In our moments of weakness, may we find refuge in your grace. Amen.

Affirmation:

"I am resilient through Christ who strengthens me. In moments of difficulty, I draw on His empowering grace, finding courage, endurance, and unwavering strength. With God as my source, I face challenges with confidence, knowing His strength is perfected in my weakness."

Gratitude

"Give thanks in all circumstances; for this is the will of God in Christ Jesus for you."

– 1 Thessalonians 5:18

"Gratitude" is a profound acknowledgment of the countless blessings that grace our lives daily. The scripture from 1 Thessalonians 5:18 serves as a guiding principle: "Give thanks in all circumstances; for this is the will of God in Christ Jesus for you." In cultivating gratitude, we align ourselves with God's divine will, recognizing that every circumstance, whether challenging or joyful, is an opportunity for heartfelt thanksgiving. Gratitude transforms our perspective, allowing us to see the hand of God at work in the intricacies of our lives.

1 Thessalonians 5:18 invites us to a continuous practice of gratitude, an acknowledgment that extends beyond favorable situations. Gratitude is a spiritual discipline that enables us to find beauty and purpose in every moment, even amidst trials. It is an expression of trust in God's sovereignty, knowing that His plan is unfolding for our good. As we offer thanks in all circumstances, we embrace a perspective that transcends the temporal and connects us to the eternal.

As we center our thoughts on the word "Gratitude" today, let us be inspired by the wisdom of 1 Thessalonians 5:18. May our hearts be filled with gratitude not just in moments of abundance but in the midst of challenges. In the act of giving thanks, we align ourselves with the divine will of God in Christ Jesus. As we express gratitude, let it become a transformative force, shaping our attitudes, fostering contentment, and deepening our connection to the source of all blessings.

Prayer:

Heavenly Father, we come before you with hearts brimming with gratitude. Teach us to give thanks in all circumstances, recognizing that your will for us is rooted in Christ Jesus. In moments of joy, we express gratitude, and in times of challenge, we trust in your plan. May our lives be a continuous offering of thanks, reflecting the profound truth that you are the source of every blessing. Amen.

Affirmation:

"I give thanks in all circumstances, for it is the will of God in Christ Jesus for me. My heart overflows with gratitude, recognizing the divine orchestration of every moment in my life. In joy and challenge alike, I choose gratitude, trusting in the goodness of God's plan."

Courage

"Be strong and courageous. Do not fear or be in dread of them, for it is the Lord your God who goes with you. He will not leave you or forsake you."

– Deuteronomy 31:6

Courage is a divine quality that emanates from the assurance of God's steadfast presence in our lives. The scripture from Deuteronomy 31:6 encapsulates this truth: "Be strong and courageous. Do not fear or be in dread of them, for it is the Lord your God who goes with you. He will not leave you or forsake you." In moments that require bravery, we are called to draw strength from our unwavering trust in God's abiding companionship. With His assurance, we find the courage to face challenges, knowing that we are never alone on our journey.

Deuteronomy 31:6 extends an invitation to cultivate courage rooted in our faith. The command to be strong and courageous is not a mere suggestion but a proclamation of the divine support that accompanies us. God's promise to never leave or forsake us becomes the bedrock of our courage. In every step we take, we do so with the confidence that the Creator of the universe is beside us, empowering us to confront fear and uncertainty with unwavering resolve.

As we meditate on the word "Courage" today, let us internalize the profound truth embedded in Deuteronomy 31:6. May our spirits be fortified with the understanding that God's presence is the wellspring of our courage. In moments of doubt or challenge, let us draw from the promise that He walks with us, providing strength beyond our own. Today, we embrace courage not as a fleeting emotion but as a divine gift, a reflection of the indomitable presence of the Lord our God.

Prayer:

Heavenly Father, grant us the courage to face each day with strength and resolve. In moments of fear or uncertainty, may we draw upon the assurance of your abiding presence. Let the truth of Deuteronomy 31:6 be etched upon our hearts, empowering us to be strong and courageous in all circumstances. We trust in your unwavering promise never to leave or forsake us. Amen.

Affirmation:

"I am strong and courageous, for the Lord my God goes with me. In moments of challenge, I draw strength from His abiding presence. Fear has no hold on me, for I trust in the promise that God will never leave nor forsake me."

Balance

> "A false balance is an abomination to the Lord, but a just weight is his delight."
>
> *– Proverbs 11:1*

Balance, as highlighted in Proverbs 11:1, is not merely a physical equilibrium but a spiritual and ethical principle that resonates with divine significance. The scripture admonishes, "A false balance is an abomination to the Lord, but a just weight is his delight." This verse invites us to cultivate balance not only in our actions but in the very essence of our being. It emphasizes the importance of integrity and fairness in all our dealings, reflecting God's desire for harmony and justice in every aspect of our lives.

Proverbs 11:1 underscores the divine pleasure found in righteousness and equity. A just weight, symbolizing fairness and equilibrium, aligns with God's character and His desire for His creation. As we strive for balance, we are called to examine the motives behind our actions, ensuring that our scales are just and not tilted by deception or self-interest. In pursuing balance, we embrace a way of living that reflects the delight of the Lord.

In contemplating the word "Balance" today, let us heed the wisdom of Proverbs 11:1. May our lives be characterized by just weights and righteous measures. As we navigate the complexities of existence, let fairness and integrity be our guiding principles. In cultivating balance, we honor the Lord and contribute to the establishment of a harmonious and just world. Let our every action be a reflection of the delight that comes from aligning our lives with the divine scales of righteousness.

Prayer:

Gracious Lord, guide us in our pursuit of balance, that our actions may reflect the just weights that delight Your heart. Keep us from false balances and lead us into a life characterized by integrity and equity. May our choices align with Your desire for harmony in all things. Amen.

Affirmation:

"I embrace balance in my life, aligning with the just weights that delight the Lord. My actions reflect fairness, integrity, and harmony, contributing to a world guided by divine principles. I am centered in God's delight as I walk in balance."

REFLECTION

Foundations of Growth Crossword Puzzle

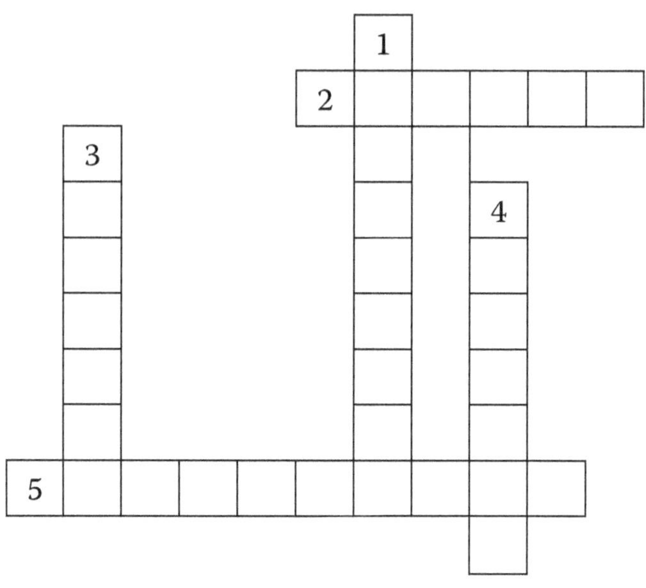

WORDS:

**GROWTH RESILIENCE GRATITUDE
COURAGE BALANCE**

ACROSS	DOWN
2. The process of increasing in size	1. The state of being grateful
5. The capacity to withstand or to recover quickly do something that frightens one from difficulties	3. The ability to 4. An even distribution of weight enabling someone or something to remain upright and steady

INTRODUCTION TO WEEK 2

Inner Clarity

Welcome to Week 2, where we delve into the transformative realm of "Inner Clarity." This week, we unravel the tapestry of words that will guide you toward a profound understanding of yourself and the world around you. The words that will illuminate your path are Clarity, Empower, Thrive, Harmony, and Innovate.

Clarity:

Our journey begins with Clarity, a beacon that pierces through the fog of confusion. Clarity is the lantern that lights the way to self-discovery, allowing you to see your purpose, values, and the essence of your being. As we explore this word, let its radiance clear the path to deeper insights and understanding.

Empower:

Empowerment is the key to unlocking your inner strength and potential. Like a phoenix rising from the ashes, you possess the ability to transform challenges into triumphs. Let empowerment infuse your journey, reminding you of the incredible power you hold within to shape your destiny.

Thrive:

Thrive, the heartbeat of this week, calls you to flourish and bloom. It's the melody of growth and abundance, encouraging you to embrace life with vitality and enthusiasm. Let the word Thrive resonate within, inspiring you to nurture your potential and live each day with purpose.

Harmony:

Harmony invites you to dance with the rhythms of life. Like a symphony coming together in perfect unity, find balance and serenity within. Embrace the interconnectedness of your experiences, relationships, and aspirations, creating a harmonious melody that resonates with your inner self.

Innovate:

Our journey concludes with the spark of Innovate, urging you to bring forth creativity and fresh perspectives. Break free from the confines of the ordinary and explore new horizons. Innovate is the catalyst that propels you towards growth, inviting you to envision a future filled with endless possibilities.

As you navigate the landscape of Inner Clarity, let these words be your companions, guiding you through self-reflection, empowerment, flourishing, harmony, and innovation. May this week unravel the layers of your inner world, providing you with the tools to cultivate a life that is not only clear but empowered, thriving, harmonious, and filled with innovation. Embrace the journey, and may the words of Week 2 resonate within your soul, bringing a deeper sense of clarity to your unlimited life.

Clarity

"For God is not a God of confusion but of peace."

– 1 Corinthians 14:33

"Clarity" is a divine illumination that dispels the shadows of confusion, aligning our hearts with the peace that comes from God. The scripture from 1 Corinthians 14:33 affirms this truth: "For God is not a God of confusion but of peace." In seeking clarity, we embark on a journey guided by the God of order, where confusion dissipates, and a tranquil sense of understanding prevails. This spiritual clarity extends beyond the intellectual realm, touching the core of our being and illuminating the path to inner peace and divine wisdom.

The verse from 1 Corinthians underscores the divine nature of clarity, reminding us that God's essence is rooted in peace and order. In our pursuit of clarity, we align ourselves with His character, seeking the tranquility that flows from a harmonious connection with the Creator. As we navigate life's complexities, clarity becomes a compass, leading us through the intricacies of decision-making, relationships, and purpose. It is an invitation to surrender confusion, trusting that God's peace will guide our steps and reveal the clarity we seek.

Today, let us meditate on the word "Clarity" and the wisdom embedded in 1 Corinthians 14:33. May our hearts be open to the divine order that brings peace, dispelling the fog of confusion. As we seek clarity in our thoughts, actions, and relationships, let us offer a prayer for divine guidance. In the stillness of our hearts, we affirm that God is a God of clarity, bringing order to every aspect of our lives.

Prayer:

Heavenly Father, we come before you seeking clarity in the midst of life's complexities. In the light of Your divine wisdom, dispel the confusion that clouds our minds. Grant us the peace that surpasses understanding as we align our hearts with Your order. May Your clarity guide our decisions and illuminate the path to Your purpose. Amen.

Affirmation:

"I embrace the divine clarity that flows from God's peace. My heart is a sanctuary of order, and confusion has no place. In alignment with 1 Corinthians 14:33, I trust in the God of clarity, and His wisdom guides my every step."

Empower

> "I can do all things through him who strengthens me."
>
> *– Philippians 4:13*

"Empower" is an invocation to recognize and embrace the limitless strength that comes from our connection with the Divine. The scripture from Philippians 4:13 encapsulates this empowerment: "I can do all things through him who strengthens me." In understanding the source of our power, we tap into a wellspring of strength that transcends human limitations. To empower ourselves is to acknowledge the divine partnership that empowers every endeavor, lifting us beyond our own capabilities.

Philippians 4:13 speaks to the profound truth that our empowerment is rooted in our relationship with God. The verse is a reminder that, through divine strength, we can navigate challenges, pursue dreams, and overcome obstacles. To empower ourselves is not an assertion of self-reliance but a declaration of dependence on the One who provides strength beyond measure. As we recognize this truth, we embark on a journey of empowerment that aligns our will with God's purpose.

Today, let us reflect on the word "Empower" and the empowering promise in Philippians 4:13. May our hearts be open to the divine strength that flows through us, enabling us to face every circumstance with courage and resilience. In our moments of self-doubt, let us offer a prayer for empowerment, acknowledging that, through Him who strengthens us, we find the capacity to do all things. In affirming this truth, we declare ourselves vessels of divine empowerment, ready to embrace the limitless possibilities within our grasp.

Prayer:

Heavenly Father, empower us with Your divine strength as we journey through life. In moments of challenge, may we draw upon the well of resilience that comes from You. Thank you for the promise in Philippians 4:13, reminding us that through You, we can do all things. Guide us on a path of empowerment, aligning our will with Yours. Amen.

Affirmation:

"I am empowered through Him who strengthens me. In every endeavor, I draw upon the limitless strength of God. Philippians 4:13 is my affirmation, and I embrace the empowerment that flows through me, achieving all things with divine strength."

Thrive

"I came that they may have life and have it abundantly."

– John 10:10

To "Thrive" is to step into the abundant life that Christ promises, as stated in John 10:10: "I came that they may have life and have it abundantly." Thriving goes beyond mere existence; it is an invitation to embrace a life overflowing with purpose, joy, and fulfillment. Christ's words are a declaration that His divine intention for us is not just survival but flourishing in every aspect of our being.

John 10:10 is a beacon of hope, guiding us toward a life of abundance. To thrive is to align our desires with God's will, tapping into the reservoir of blessings He offers. It is an affirmation that, through Christ, we are destined for richness of life—spiritually, emotionally, and materially. Thriving is not a selfish pursuit but a recognition that, in embracing God's abundance, we become vessels of His love and grace.

As we contemplate the word "Thrive," let us meditate on the profound truth in John 10:10. May our hearts be open to the abundant life Christ offers, and may we actively seek ways to thrive in His grace. In our pursuit of purpose, joy, and fulfillment, let us offer a prayer for divine guidance. With gratitude, we affirm the promise of John 10:10 and declare our intention to live a life that thrives in the abundance of Christ.

Prayer:

Heavenly Father, thank you for the promise of abundant life through Your Son, Jesus Christ. Guide us on a path where we not only survive but thrive in Your grace. May our lives be a testament to the richness of Your blessings, and may we embrace the abundant life You offer. Lead us in purpose, joy, and fulfillment. Amen.

Affirmation:

"I thrive in the abundant life promised by Christ. John 10:10 is my affirmation, and I embrace the richness of God's blessings. In Him, I live a life that flourishes in purpose, joy, and fulfillment, reflecting the abundance of His grace."

Harmony

> "Strive for peace with everyone, and for the holiness without which no one will see the Lord."
>
> *– Hebrews 12:14*

"Harmony" is a divine symphony where the melody of peace intertwines with the pursuit of holiness. Hebrews 12:14 guides us on this harmonious journey: "Strive for peace with everyone, and for the holiness without which no one will see the Lord." Harmony is not merely the absence of conflict but a conscious effort to foster peace in our relationships, coupled with a commitment to a life characterized by holiness. It is an invitation to create a harmonious atmosphere where the presence of the Lord is not only sought but genuinely felt.

Hebrews 12:14 encourages us to actively seek peace and holiness, recognizing their interdependence. Harmony is the result of intentional efforts to reconcile with others and to live a life that reflects the holiness of our Creator. As we strive for peace, we contribute to the establishment of God's kingdom on earth—a realm characterized by harmonious relationships and a pursuit of holiness that draws us closer to the Lord. Harmony, in this context, becomes a sacred commitment to reflect God's nature in our interactions.

Today, let us reflect on the word "Harmony" and the guidance provided in Hebrews 12:14. May our hearts be attuned to the call for peace and holiness, recognizing them as integral components of a harmonious life. In our pursuit of harmonious relationships and a holy existence, let us offer a prayer for divine assistance. As we strive for peace and holiness, may our lives become a testament to the presence of the Lord in our midst.

Prayer:

Gracious God, guide us on the path of harmony, where peace and holiness converge. Grant us the strength to strive for peace with everyone and the discipline to pursue holiness. May our lives be a reflection of Your divine nature, and may we create an atmosphere where Your presence is felt. Amen.

Affirmation:

"I strive for harmony in my relationships, seeking peace with everyone. In tandem, I pursue holiness, knowing it brings me closer to the Lord. Hebrews 12:14 is my guide, and in harmony with God's will, I create a sacred space where His presence is evident."

Innovate

> "Behold, I am doing a new thing; now it springs forth, do you not perceive it? I will make a way in the wilderness and rivers in the desert."
>
> *– Isaiah 43:19*

To "Innovate" is to align ourselves with the divine creativity that Isaiah 43:19 unveils: "Behold, I am doing a new thing; now it springs forth, do you not perceive it?" Innovation is not merely a human endeavor; it is an acknowledgment of God's continuous act of creating and making all things new. As we engage in the process of innovation, we participate in the unfolding of God's plan, perceiving and embracing the new possibilities He brings forth.

Isaiah 43:19 is a profound invitation to recognize the hand of God in innovation. It assures us that, even in seemingly barren places, God will make a way. Innovation is a journey where we trust in God's ability to create opportunities, pathways, and solutions that defy human expectations. It is a partnership with the Creator, who fashions new things out of the raw materials of our lives, making a way even in the wilderness and rivers in the desert of our circumstances.

Today, as we focus on the word "Innovate," let us meditate on the promise found in Isaiah 43:19. May our hearts be open to the new things God is doing in our lives and in the world around us. As we embark on innovative endeavors, let us offer a prayer for divine guidance and inspiration. In aligning our creativity with God's, may we perceive the newness springing forth and trust in His ability to make a way where there seems to be none.

Prayer:

Creator God, thank you for the promise of new things unfolding in our lives. As we innovate, we seek Your guidance and inspiration. Open our eyes to perceive the newness springing forth, and grant us the courage to trust in Your ability to make a way in every circumstance. May our innovative efforts align with Your divine plan. Amen.

Affirmation:

"I am an innovator, aligned with God's creative spirit. Isaiah 43:19 is my inspiration, and I perceive the new things God is doing. In every innovative endeavor, I trust in His ability to make a way, even in the wilderness and rivers in the desert."

REFLECTION

Focus Moment

Clarity:

Explore moments in your day where you felt a sense of clarity or confusion. What contributed to or hindered your understanding?

____

____

Empower:

Identify instances where you felt empowered or disempowered. What actions or mindset led to these feelings?

____

____

Thrive:

Reflect on areas where you thrived or encountered challenges. What lessons can you draw from both experiences?

____

____

Harmony:

Consider the balance in your life. Where did you find harmony, and where might adjustments be beneficial?

____

____

Innovate:

Explore opportunities where you embraced innovation or creativity. How can you bring more innovation into your life?

____

____

This exercise can help you gain deeper insights into your thoughts, emotions, and behaviors. It serves as a compass for navigating the complexities of life and empowers you to make intentional choices aligned with your personal growth journey.

You are doing great!

INTRODUCTION TO WEEK 3

Transformative Power

Step into Week 3, where we explore the potent domain of "Transformative Power." This week's words—Transform, Persevere, Wisdom, Reflect, and Adapt—unfold as catalysts for profound change and personal evolution. Prepare to harness the transformative power within and around you.

Transform:

Our journey begins with the word Transform, inviting you to embrace change as a powerful force. Like a caterpillar becoming a butterfly, allow transformation to shape your journey. Recognize that each moment is an opportunity for growth and renewal, unfolding the wings of your unlimited potential.

Persevere:

Persevere, the steadfast companion, propels you forward in the face of challenges. Just as a resilient tree weathers storms, your perseverance is the anchor that ensures growth. Let this word echo in your spirit, reminding you that every hurdle is a stepping stone toward your desired transformation.

Wisdom:

Wisdom illuminates the path, guiding your transformative journey with discernment and insight. As you explore this word, seek the profound understanding that comes from experiences and reflections. May wisdom be the compass, directing you toward choices that align with your highest self.

Reflect:

Reflection becomes a sacred mirror this week, allowing you to gaze inward. Like a serene pond mirroring the sky, take moments to reflect on your experiences, thoughts, and aspirations. Through reflection, discover the hidden gems that contribute to your ongoing transformation.

Adapt:

Adapt, the versatile ally, encourages you to dance with the rhythm of change. Like a river that molds itself around obstacles, allow adaptability to be your strength. Embrace the notion that adaptability is not just a survival skill but a powerful tool for shaping a purposeful and transformative life.

As you embark on this week's exploration of Transformative Power, let these words become the threads weaving a tapestry of change and growth. May Transform, Persevere, Wisdom, Reflect, and Adapt infuse your days with resilience, insight, introspection, and flexibility. Embrace the transformative power within you and witness the beauty that unfolds on this extraordinary journey. Welcome to a week where your own transformative power takes center stage.

Transform

> "Do not be conformed to this world, but be transformed by the renewal of your mind, that by testing you may discern what is the will of God, what is good and acceptable and perfect."
>
> *– Romans 12:2*

To "Transform" is to heed the wisdom of Romans 12:2, which urges us not to conform to the patterns of the world but to undergo a renewal of the mind. Transformation is a sacred process that involves shedding the influences of the world and embracing a renewed perspective shaped by the divine. It is an intentional journey where our minds are aligned with God's truth, leading us away from conformity and towards a state of being that reflects His will.

Romans 12:2 highlights the transformative power of renewing our minds. It is a call to discern the will of God through testing and refining our understanding. Transformation is not a one-time event but a continuous process of aligning our thoughts with the divine, allowing us to discern what is good, acceptable, and perfect in His sight. As we transform, we become vessels of God's will, reflecting His values and purposes in our lives.

Today, let us meditate on the word "Transform" and the guidance found in Romans 12:2. May our minds be open to renewal, and may we actively seek transformation in alignment with God's will. As we embark on this journey, let us offer a prayer for divine guidance and a discerning spirit. May our transformation be a testament to the goodness, acceptability, and perfection found in living according to God's design.

Prayer:

Heavenly Father, guide us on the path of transformation as we renew our minds according to Your will. Grant us the discernment to test and understand what is good, acceptable, and perfect in Your sight. May our lives be a reflection of the transformative power of Your truth. Amen.

Affirmation:

"I am on a transformative journey, renewing my mind according to God's will. Romans 12:2 is my guide, and through continuous testing, I discern what is good, acceptable, and perfect. My transformation reflects the divine pattern in my life."

Persevere

"Blessed is the man who remains steadfast under trial, for when he has stood the test, he will receive the crown of life, which God has promised to those who love him."

– James 1:12

To "Persevere" is to embrace the blessing pronounced in James 1:12—a blessing reserved for those who remain steadfast under trials. Perseverance is not merely enduring challenges but standing firm with unwavering faith in God's promises. The scripture reminds us that in the face of trials, a blessed reward awaits those who persevere—a crown of life, a testament to the resilience of a heart that loves and trusts God.

James 1:12 extols the virtue of perseverance under trial. It is a call to navigate challenges with enduring faith, knowing that trials are not without purpose. Perseverance is not a solitary struggle but a journey where we stand the test with God as our constant companion. As we persevere, we are promised a crown of life—a symbol of victory over adversity and a testimony to our love and devotion to the Creator.

As we reflect on the word "Persevere" today, let us internalize the promise in James 1:12. May our hearts be fortified with the understanding that trials are opportunities for growth, and perseverance is the key to receiving the crown of life. In moments of challenge, let us offer a prayer for strength and resilience. May our perseverance be an act of love for God, trusting that His promises endure and bring forth blessings in due time.

Prayer:

Heavenly Father, grant us the strength to persevere under trial, knowing that You are with us in every challenge. In moments of difficulty, help us stand the test with unwavering faith and endurance. May our perseverance be an expression of our love for You. We trust in Your promise of the crown of life for those who remain steadfast. Amen.

Affirmation:

"I am blessed as I persevere under trials. James 1:12 is my assurance that, when I stand the test with unwavering faith, I will receive the crown of life. My perseverance is an act of love for God, and His promises are my anchor."

Wisdom

"The fear of the Lord is the beginning of wisdom, and the knowledge of the Holy One is insight."

– Proverbs 9:10

To seek "Wisdom" is to embark on a journey rooted in reverence for the Lord, as Proverbs 9:10 declares: "The fear of the Lord is the beginning of wisdom." True wisdom finds its foundation in acknowledging God's sovereignty and aligning our hearts with His divine principles. It is not merely intellectual knowledge but a deep, reverent understanding that positions us on the path of true wisdom—a path that begins with awe and respect for the Creator.

Proverbs 9:10 teaches us that wisdom is not separate from the knowledge of the Holy One. It is an insight born out of a relationship with God. As we draw near to Him, seeking to know Him intimately, we gain a profound understanding that transcends human intellect. Wisdom, in this context, is a sacred illumination that enables us to navigate life with discernment and clarity, grounded in the knowledge of the Holy One.

As we focus on the word "Wisdom" today, let us meditate on the wisdom found in Proverbs 9:10. May our hearts be open to the fear of the Lord as the wellspring of true wisdom. In our pursuit of knowledge, let us offer a prayer for a deepening relationship with the Holy One. May our lives be characterized by the wisdom that emanates from reverence, and may our actions reflect the divine insight that comes from knowing the Lord intimately.

Prayer:

Heavenly Father, grant us the wisdom that begins with the fear of the Lord. May our hearts be filled with reverence for Your sovereignty.

As we seek knowledge of the Holy One, deepen our understanding and insight. Guide us on a path where true wisdom is cultivated, and may our lives be a testament to the transformative power of divine knowledge. Amen.

Affirmation:

"I seek wisdom that begins with the fear of the Lord. Proverbs 9:10 is my guide, and in the knowledge of the Holy One, I find true insight. My life is grounded in reverence, and divine wisdom illuminates my path."

Reflect

"But be doers of the word, and not hearers only, deceiving yourselves."

– James 1:22

To "Reflect" is to heed the wisdom of James 1:22—a call not merely to hear the word but to be active doers of it. Reflection, in this context, is not a passive contemplation but an intentional engagement with the teachings of the Word. James invites us to go beyond hearing, emphasizing the importance of embodying the truth we encounter. Reflecting is a transformative act that moves us from self-deception to genuine alignment with the principles of God's Word.

James 1:22 serves as a reminder that true understanding comes through action. To reflect on the Word is to internalize its teachings and allow them to shape our behavior. It is an intentional process of incorporating God's truth into the fabric of our lives, ensuring that our actions align with our beliefs. Reflection is a bridge between hearing and doing, a transformative journey that propels us from knowledge to active obedience.

As we consider the word "Reflect" today, let us meditate on the wisdom found in James 1:22. May our reflection on the Word be a catalyst for action, preventing self-deception and leading us towards genuine transformation. In moments of introspection, let us offer a prayer for guidance and a heart willing to be shaped by the Word. May our lives be a testament to the power of reflective obedience, as we move beyond hearing to actively living out the truths of God's Word.

Prayer:

Gracious God, guide us in our reflection on Your Word. May our hearts be receptive to the transformative power of Your teachings. As we consider the truths revealed to us, grant us the strength and willingness to be doers of the Word. Guard us against self-deception, and may our lives reflect the active obedience that stems from a genuine understanding of Your truth. Amen.

Affirmation:

"I reflect on the Word not as a passive observer but as an active doer. James 1:22 is my guide, and I embody the truths I encounter. My reflection leads to transformation, and my actions align with the wisdom of God's Word."

Adapt

"I have become all things to all people, that by all means I might save some."

– 1 Corinthians 9:22

To "Adapt" is to embody the ethos of 1 Corinthians 9:22, where the Apostle Paul expresses his willingness to become all things to all people for the sake of saving some. Adaptation, in the Christian context, is not about compromising one's core beliefs but about connecting with others in ways that resonate with their experiences. It is a call to empathize, understand, and engage with diverse perspectives, demonstrating a Christ-like love that transcends cultural and personal barriers.

1 Corinthians 9:22 encourages a mindset of adaptability for the higher purpose of salvation. The verse reflects a commitment to meet people where they are, embracing various cultural contexts to effectively share the Gospel. Adaptation is an intentional choice to break down barriers and communicate God's love in ways that are accessible and relatable. It requires a deep understanding of the diverse needs and backgrounds of those we seek to reach.

As we contemplate the word "Adapt" today, let us reflect on the spirit of 1 Corinthians 9:22. May our hearts be open to the call of adaptation for the sake of the Gospel. In our interactions with others, let us offer a prayer for humility and understanding. May our lives be characterized by a Christ-like adaptability that fosters connection, breaks down barriers, and opens doors for the transformative message of salvation.

Prayer:

Gracious Lord, grant us the wisdom to adapt our approach for the sake of sharing Your love and salvation. May our hearts be open to diverse perspectives, and may we connect with others in ways that resonate with their experiences. Guide us in humility that we may become all things to all people for the higher purpose of saving souls. Amen.

Affirmation:

"I embrace the spirit of adaptation for the sake of the Gospel. 1 Corinthians 9:22 is my inspiration, and I willingly become all things to all people to share the transformative message of God's love and salvation. My adaptability reflects Christ's inclusive and compassionate love."

REFLECTION

Transformative Power Word Search

H	E	T	R	A	N	S	F	O	R	M	D	K	P	R
P	V	P	V	K	X	U	N	Y	D	P	A	V	S	W
R	E	K	B	F	U	K	H	V	G	O	L	I	V	A
U	T	R	L	O	A	X	H	S	V	T	Y	J	J	G
A	P	R	S	X	Z	X	S	N	H	V	R	E	L	O
W	O	X	T	E	J	U	A	V	F	J	U	P	H	J
I	E	F	N	O	V	N	S	D	C	A	N	A	R	U
S	T	B	E	O	U	E	F	W	R	Q	J	A	T	M
D	P	V	B	L	O	V	R	T	E	N	V	Q	I	L
O	A	F	X	G	S	A	V	E	F	N	O	F	E	T
M	B	M	A	O	G	D	E	U	L	C	K	T	N	C
G	Q	O	E	H	Z	A	Q	D	E	P	H	J	N	H
M	W	T	J	Z	E	P	D	V	C	N	P	Z	X	F
B	B	O	P	Z	S	T	X	Z	T	B	M	W	S	Q
W	K	S	Q	T	G	S	Q	Y	Z	O	M	U	N	D

WORDS:

TRANSFORM PERSEVERE REFLECT WISDOM ADAPT

INTRODUCTION TO WEEK 4

Visionary Living

Step into Week 4, where we embark on a journey of "Visionary Living." This week, the words—Vision, Abundance, Integrity, Patience, and Optimize—invite you to envision a life filled with purpose, integrity, and an abundance of meaningful experiences. Get ready to cultivate a visionary approach to living.

Vision:

Our exploration begins with Vision, the compass that guides your life's direction. Just as a captain navigates by the stars, let your vision be the guiding light illuminating your path. Envision the life you desire and allow your aspirations to shape the journey ahead.

Abundance:

Abundance is the heartbeat of this week, urging you to recognize the richness that surrounds you. Like a garden flourishing with diverse blooms, acknowledge the abundance in your life—love, opportunities, and blessings. Let an attitude of abundance color your perception, fostering gratitude and contentment.

Integrity:

Integrity, the cornerstone of visionary living, invites you to align your actions with your values. Just as a sturdy bridge stands true, let integrity be the foundation of your character. Embrace honesty, authenticity, and ethical choices, creating a life built on a solid and trustworthy framework.

Patience:

Patience becomes your serene companion, encouraging you to trust the timing of your journey. Like a gardener awaiting the bloom of a flower, cultivate patience as you navigate life's seasons. Trust that each moment unfolds in its own time, contributing to the grand tapestry of your visionary life.

Optimize:

Optimize, the final brushstroke in our visionary palette, calls you to refine and enhance your daily experiences. Like a sculptor molding clay into a masterpiece, seek to optimize various aspects of your life—relationships, habits, and endeavors. Strive for efficiency and effectiveness in your pursuits, creating a canvas of optimized living.

As you delve into Visionary Living this week, may these words inspire you to create a life that reflects your deepest values and aspirations. Let Vision, Abundance, Integrity, Patience, and Optimize weave together, painting a vibrant picture of a life lived with purpose, abundance, and authenticity. Welcome to a week where your vision for living unfolds with each intentional step.

Vision

> "Where there is no prophetic vision, the people cast off restraint, but blessed is he who keeps the law."
>
> *– Proverbs 29:18*

To have "Vision" is to embrace the wisdom of Proverbs 29:18, acknowledging the power of prophetic insight in guiding and uniting a people. The verse warns that without a clear vision, people cast off restraint. Vision, in this context, is not just foresight but a divinely inspired perspective that provides direction, purpose, and a moral compass for collective behavior. It is a call to seek and understand the prophetic vision that aligns with God's principles.

Proverbs 29:18 emphasizes the importance of keeping the law as a source of blessing. Vision is not divorced from obedience; rather, it flourishes when individuals and communities align themselves with God's law. It is a call to both receive and actively participate in the divine vision, ensuring that it doesn't lead to chaos but becomes a source of blessing. Vision, coupled with adherence to God's law, creates a framework for a blessed and purposeful life.

As we ponder the word "Vision" today, let us reflect on the guidance found in Proverbs 29:18. May our hearts be open to prophetic insight that aligns with God's law. In our pursuit of divine vision, let us offer a prayer for discernment and a commitment to keeping His commandments. May our lives be characterized by a visionary obedience that leads to blessing, purpose, and alignment with God's divine plan.

Prayer:

Heavenly Father, grant us the discernment to embrace prophetic vision that aligns with Your law. May our hearts be open to the direction and purpose Your vision provides. As we seek clarity, help us keep Your commandments, that our lives may be a source of blessing. Guide us in obedience to Your divine vision. Amen.

Affirmation:

"I embrace the prophetic vision that aligns with God's law. Proverbs 29:18 is my guide, and I actively participate in keeping His commandments. My life is characterized by purpose, direction, and the blessings that flow from visionary obedience."

Abundance

"The thief comes only to steal and kill and destroy. I came that they may have life and have it abundantly."

– John 10:10

To experience "Abundance" is to understand the profound contrast illustrated in John 10:10—a juxtaposition of the thief's destructive intentions and Christ's promise of abundant life. Abundance, in the context of this verse, is not merely a surplus of material possessions but a richness that encompasses every facet of life. It is a promise of vitality, purpose, and fulfillment that transcends the thief's attempts to steal, kill, and destroy.

John 10:10 highlights Jesus' mission to offer abundant life. Abundance, according to Christ, is the antithesis of the thief's malevolent intentions. It is a life filled with the goodness and blessings that flow from a deep connection with the Creator. This abundance is not contingent upon external circumstances but is rooted in a spiritual reality that transcends the temporal challenges posed by the thief.

As we contemplate the word "Abundance" today, let us reflect on the promise embedded in John 10:10. May our understanding of abundance extend beyond the material realm to encompass spiritual richness, purpose, and vitality. In our pursuit of abundant life, let us offer a prayer for gratitude and a heart attuned to the abundance Christ offers. May our lives be a testament to the transformative power of His promise—a life abundant in every dimension.

Prayer:

Gracious Lord, thank you for the promise of abundant life through Your Son, Jesus Christ. Protect us from the thief's destructive intentions, and may our lives be filled with the richness and blessings that come from a deep connection with You. Open our hearts to receive the abundance You offer in every aspect of life. Amen.

53

Affirmation:

"I embrace the promise of abundance in John 10:10. My life is safeguarded from the thief's intentions, and I walk in the richness, purpose, and vitality that Christ offers. Abundance is my reality, and I receive it with gratitude and open-hearted joy."

Integrity

"The integrity of the upright guides them, but the crooked-ness of the treacherous destroys them."

– Proverbs 11:3

To embody "Integrity" is to heed the wisdom of Proverbs 11:3—a recognition that the moral compass of the upright guides their actions. Integrity, in this context, is not just an adherence to moral principles but a guiding force that directs individuals along a path of righteousness. It is a virtue that leads the upright in a manner consistent with honesty, fairness, and ethical conduct.

Proverbs 11:3 emphasizes the destructive consequences of crooked-ness and treachery. Integrity serves as a protective shield for the upright, guiding them away from actions that could lead to their own destruction. It is a beacon of light that illuminates the path of righteousness, deterring the treacherous from the pitfalls of deceit and dishonesty.

As we reflect on the word "Integrity" today, let us meditate on the guidance found in Proverbs 11:3. May our hearts be open to the influence of integrity, serving as a moral compass in our decisions and actions. In our pursuit of upright living, let us offer a prayer for strength and a commitment to ethical conduct. May our lives be characterized by the integrity that guides us and protects us from the destructive consequences of treachery.

Prayer:

Heavenly Father, grant us the strength to uphold integrity in our actions and decisions. May our hearts be guided by the moral com-pass of righteousness. Protect us from the destructive consequences of crookedness and treachery. As we navigate life, may integrity be a constant companion, leading us along the path of honesty and fairness. Amen.

Affirmation:

"I embrace the virtue of integrity, guided by the wisdom of Proverbs 11:3. My actions are aligned with righteousness, and I am protected from the destructive consequences of deceit. Integrity is my moral compass, leading me in the path of honesty and fairness."

Patience

"But if we hope for what we do not see, we wait for it with patience."

– Romans 8:25

To practice "Patience" is to embrace the wisdom of Romans 8:25—a recognition that genuine hope is accompanied by the virtue of waiting with patience. Patience, in this context, is not a passive endurance but an active trust in the fulfillment of our hopes. It is a virtue that allows us to navigate the uncertainties of life with a steadfast confidence that what we hope for will come to fruition.

Romans 8:25 highlights the inseparable connection between hope and patience. True hope, according to this verse, involves an enduring patience in the face of unseen outcomes. Patience is the soil in which hope takes root and grows into a resilient expectancy. It is an acknowledgment that some of the most valuable things in life require time to unfold, and the journey of waiting is an integral part of the process.

As we contemplate the word "Patience" today, let us reflect on the guidance found in Romans 8:25. May our hearts be open to the virtue of patience as we navigate the unknowns of life. In our moments of hope, let us offer a prayer for enduring patience and a trust that what we do not see will unfold in its appointed time. May our lives be characterized by a patient hope that strengthens us on the journey.

Prayer:

Gracious Lord, grant us the virtue of patience as we hope for unseen outcomes. May our hearts be steadfast in waiting with confidence. In moments of uncertainty, help us cultivate enduring patience, trusting that what we hope for will manifest in its appointed time. Guide us in a patient hope that strengthens our faith. Amen.

Affirmation:

"I cultivate the virtue of patience in my journey of hope. Romans 8:25 is my guide, and I wait with confidence for the unseen to unfold. Patience is my strength, and in its embrace, I trust that what I hope for will manifest in its appointed time."

Optimize

> "So, whether you eat or drink, or whatever you do, do all to the glory of God."
>
> *– 1 Corinthians 10:31*

To "Optimize" is to align with the directive in 1 Corinthians 10:31—a call to do all things for the glory of God. Optimization, in this context, transcends mere efficiency; it is a conscious effort to elevate every aspect of life to a level that reflects and magnifies God's glory. It is an invitation to cultivate a mindset where even the seemingly mundane activities are opportunities for worship and service to the Creator.

1 Corinthians 10:31 underscores the universal scope of optimization—whether in eating, drinking, or any other action, the purpose remains to glorify God. Optimization becomes a holistic approach to life, where every choice and action is intentional and aligned with the divine purpose. It is a reminder that our lives are interconnected, and through optimization, we weave a tapestry of devotion that glorifies God in all spheres.

As we consider the word "Optimize" today, let us meditate on the guidance found in 1 Corinthians 10:31. May our hearts be open to the holistic approach of optimizing our lives for God's glory. In our daily activities, let us offer a prayer for intentionality and a commitment to do all things in a manner that magnifies the Creator. May our lives be a symphony of optimization, harmonizing with the divine purpose in every aspect.

Prayer:

Heavenly Father, guide us in the journey of optimization, where every aspect of our lives is aligned with the purpose of glorifying

You. May our choices and actions be intentional, reflecting a heart devoted to Your glory. In moments of decision-making, help us optimize our lives for Your honor. Amen.

59

Affirmation:

"I optimize every aspect of my life for the glory of God. 1 Corinthians 10:31 is my guide, and in eating, drinking, and all actions, I am intentional in reflecting the Creator's magnificence. My life is optimized for His honor, weaving a tapestry of devotion in every sphere."

REFLECTION

<u>Visionary Living Crossword Puzzle</u>

<u>WORDS:</u>

**VISION   ABUNDANCE   INTEGRITY
PATIENCE   OPTIMIZE**

ACROSS:

2. A very large quantity of something
3. The ability to accept delay, suffering, or annoyance without complaining or becoming angry
5. To make as perfect, effective, or functional as possible

DOWN:

1. The quality of being honest and having strong moral principles that you refuse to change
4. The faculty or state of being able to see

Empathetic Connection

Enter Week 5, where the theme is "Empathetic Connection." This transformative week revolves around the words—Empathy, Discipline, Explore, Flourish, and Inspire—guiding you toward a deeper understanding of human connections, self-discipline, and the inspiration that fuels a flourishing life.

Empathy:

Our exploration begins with Empathy, the bridge that connects hearts and fosters understanding. Like a gentle rain that nourishes the earth, let empathy be the force that nurtures compassion within you. Explore the power of shared emotions and the transformative impact of walking in someone else's shoes.

Discipline:

Discipline becomes the steady rhythm underlining empathic connection. Like a skilled musician practicing their instrument, embrace the discipline needed to cultivate meaningful relationships. Discipline in actions and thoughts strengthens the bonds you share, fostering an environment where empathy can thrive.

Explore:

Explore invites you to venture into the realms of others' experiences. Like an intrepid traveler discovering new landscapes, open your heart to diverse perspectives. Through exploration, you expand your capacity for empathy, discovering the beauty and richness that different narratives bring to the tapestry of human connection.

Flourish:

Flourish is the vibrant blossom of empathic living. Like a garden thriving with diverse flora, let your relationships and personal growth flourish. Cultivate an environment where understanding and support create a fertile ground for empathy to blossom, contributing to the vibrant tapestry of your life.

Inspire:

Inspire, the final note in this symphony, calls you to be a source of encouragement and motivation. Like a beacon lighting the way, let your actions and words inspire those around you. Through empathy, discipline, exploration, and flourishing connections, become a catalyst for positive change and inspiration.

As you immerse yourself in the week of Empathetic Connection, may these words guide you toward deeper understanding, disciplined connection, and the inspiration that emanates from empathetic living. Let Empathy, Discipline, Explore, Flourish, and Inspire become the threads weaving a tapestry of rich, meaningful relationships and a life inspired by the beauty of human connection. Welcome to a week where empathy forms the foundation of transformative connections.

Empathy

"Finally, all of you, have unity of mind, sympathy, brotherly love, a tender heart, and a humble mind."

– 1 Peter 3:8

To practice "Empathy" is to embody the virtues outlined in 1 Peter 3:8—a call to unity, sympathy, brotherly love, a tender heart, and a humble mind. Empathy, in this context, is not a passive acknowledgment of others' feelings but an active engagement with their experiences. It is a commitment to understanding, sharing, and expressing genuine compassion in unity with our fellow beings.

1 Peter 3:8 provides a comprehensive blueprint for empathetic living. Unity of mind fosters a sense of interconnectedness, while sympathy calls us to feel with others in their joys and sorrows. Brotherly love transcends mere affection, emphasizing a deep, familial bond. A tender heart reflects the compassion necessary for empathetic connection, and a humble mind acknowledges the equality of all humanity. Empathy, as outlined, is a holistic and transformative way of relating to others.

As we reflect on the word "Empathy" today, let us meditate on the virtues presented in 1 Peter 3:8. May our hearts be open to the practice of empathy in our interactions with others. In moments of unity, sympathy, and brotherly love, let us offer a prayer for a tender heart and a humble mind. May our lives be characterized by the transformative power of empathy, fostering genuine connections and understanding.

Prayer:

Merciful God, grant us the grace to embody empathy in our relationships. May our hearts be attuned to unity, sympathy, brotherly love, tenderness, and humility. In moments of interaction, help us practice empathy, understanding, and compassion. May our lives be a testament to the transformative power of empathetic living. Amen.

Affirmation:

"I embrace empathy in my interactions with others. 1 Peter 3:8 guides me to unity, sympathy, brotherly love, a tender heart, and a humble mind. My life is a reflection of genuine compassion, fostering connections and understanding with those around me."

Discipline

"For the moment all discipline seems painful rather than pleasant, but later it yields the peaceful fruit of righteousness to those who have been trained by it."

– Hebrews 12:11

To embody "Discipline" is to embrace the wisdom found in Hebrews 12:11—a recognition that discipline, though initially challenging, bears the promise of yielding the peaceful fruit of righteousness. Discipline, in this context, is not solely punitive but a transformative process that molds and refines character. It is a commitment to intentional growth, even in the face of momentary discomfort.

Hebrews 12:11 acknowledges the immediate challenges of discipline, emphasizing the contrast between short-term pain and the enduring fruit it bears. Discipline, whether in physical, spiritual, or emotional realms, serves as a refining fire that shapes individuals into vessels of righteousness. It is an investment in long-term growth, promising a harvest of peace and righteousness for those who endure the training.

As we reflect on the word "Discipline" today, let us meditate on the guidance offered in Hebrews 12:11. May our hearts be open to the transformative power of disciplined living, understanding that the momentary discomfort paves the way for lasting peace and righteousness. In moments of discipline, let us offer a prayer for endurance and a commitment to growth. May our lives be a testament to the peaceful fruits that discipline yields in those who have been trained by it.

Prayer:

Heavenly Father, grant us the strength to endure the discipline that leads to growth and righteousness. May our hearts be open to the transformative process of discipline, recognizing its role in shaping our character. In moments of challenge, help us persevere, knowing that the peaceful fruit of righteousness awaits those who have been trained by discipline. Amen.

Affirmation:

"I embrace discipline as a transformative process. Hebrews 12:11 guides me through momentary challenges, knowing that the peaceful fruit of righteousness awaits. My life is a testament to the enduring growth that disciplined living brings, and I walk in the path of lasting peace."

Explore

> "Ask, and it will be given to you; seek, and you will find; knock, and it will be opened to you."
>
> *– Matthew 7:7*

To "Explore" is to heed the invitation of Matthew 7:7—a call to ask, seek, and knock with the expectation of receiving, finding, and having doors opened. Exploration, in this context, is not merely a physical journey but a spiritual and intellectual pursuit. It is an active engagement with life's mysteries, fueled by curiosity and a desire for discovery. The verse encourages a proactive approach to exploration, recognizing that the quest for understanding and growth requires intentional effort.

Matthew 7:7 underscores the principle of reciprocity in exploration. Asking involves an open and inquisitive mind, seeking requires a determined pursuit of knowledge or experience, and knocking implies an active engagement with opportunities. The verse assures that such intentional exploration will be met with corresponding outcomes—receiving, finding, and doors opening.

As we contemplate the word "Explore" today, let us meditate on the guidance found in Matthew 7:7. May our hearts be open to the spirit of exploration, whether in our spiritual journey, intellectual pursuits, or personal growth. In moments of asking, seeking, and knocking, let us offer a prayer for guidance and a commitment to intentional exploration. May our lives be characterized by a spirit of curiosity and discovery, knowing that as we explore, we will receive, find, and have doors opened.

Prayer:

Gracious God, guide us in the spirit of exploration, as encouraged in Matthew 7:7. May our hearts be open to asking, seeking, and knocking in our spiritual and intellectual pursuits. Grant us the courage to explore with intentionality, knowing that the rewards of receiving, finding, and having doors opened await those who actively engage in the journey. Amen.

Affirmation:

"I embrace the spirit of exploration in my journey. Matthew 7:7 is my guide, and as I ask, seek, and knock with intentionality, I am open to receiving, finding, and having doors opened. My life is a continual exploration, filled with curiosity, growth, and discovery."

Flourish

"The righteous flourish like the palm tree and grow like a cedar in Lebanon."

– Psalm 92:12

To "Flourish" is to align with the imagery presented in Psalm 92:12—a picturesque depiction of the righteous flourishing like palm trees and growing like cedars in Lebanon. Flourishing, in this context, transcends mere survival; it is a vibrant and fruitful existence that emanates from a righteous life. It is a call to thrive and grow, rooted in a deep connection with God's principles.

Psalm 92:12 draws upon the strength and resilience of palm trees and the majestic growth of cedars. The righteous, likened to these symbols, are portrayed as resilient and majestic in their spiritual and personal growth. Flourishing becomes a testament to the transformative power of righteousness, enabling individuals to weather the storms of life and stand tall in spiritual stature.

As we reflect on the word "Flourish" today, let us meditate on the vibrant imagery found in Psalm 92:12. May our hearts be open to the transformative power of righteousness, allowing us to flourish like palm trees and grow like cedars. In moments of reflection, let us offer a prayer for spiritual resilience and growth. May our lives be a testament to the flourishing that comes from aligning with God's principles.

Prayer:

Heavenly Father, grant us the grace to flourish in righteousness, as described in Psalm 92:12. May our lives be vibrant and fruitful, resilient like palm trees, and majestic like cedars. In moments of growth, help us to deepen our connection with You. May our lives be characterized by flourishing, a testimony to the transformative power of righteousness. Amen.

Affirmation:

"I embrace the call to flourish in righteousness. Psalm 92:12 is my guide, and as I align with God's principles, I flourish like palm trees and grow like cedars. My life is vibrant, resilient, and majestic—a testament to the transformative power of righteousness."

Inspire

> "Let no one despise you for your youth, but set the believers an example in speech, in conduct, in love, in faith, in purity."
>
> *– 1 Timothy 4:12*

To "Inspire" is to heed the counsel of 1 Timothy 4:12—a reminder that youth should not be a hindrance but an opportunity to set an example in various facets of life. Inspiration, in this context, is a call to be a source of encouragement and motivation through the way one speaks, behaves, loves, believes, and lives a life of purity. It is an acknowledgment that regardless of age, one can be a beacon of light and influence.

1 Timothy 4:12 emphasizes the power of example-setting. The verse challenges individuals, especially the youth, to rise above stereotypes and societal expectations. To inspire is not just to talk about ideals but to embody them. It is a call to be a living testament to the transformative power of faith, love, and purity, setting a standard that encourages others to follow.

As we contemplate the word "Inspire" today, let us meditate on the guidance found in 1 Timothy 4:12. May our hearts be open to the responsibility and privilege of setting an example. In moments of interaction with others, let us offer a prayer for guidance and a commitment to inspiring those around us. May our lives be characterized by a spirit of encouragement and a living example that transcends age or circumstance.

Prayer:

Gracious Lord, guide us in the responsibility to inspire others, as encouraged in 1 Timothy 4:12. May our words, actions, love, faith, and purity set an example that transcends age or circumstance. In moments of interaction, help us inspire those around us, being a source of encouragement and motivation. Amen.

Affirmation:

"I embrace the call to inspire through example. 1 Timothy 4:12 is my guide, and in speech, conduct, love, faith, and purity, I set an example that transcends age. My life is a source of encouragement and motivation, inspiring others to embrace transformative ideals."

REFLECTION

Here are some empathy exercises that can be incorporate into your daily life to enhance empathetic connections alone with prayer and discernment:

Reflective Listening:

Practice active listening by fully focusing on what the other person is saying without interrupting.

Reflect back what you've heard to ensure understanding before responding.

Role Reversal:

Choose a recent interaction and mentally place yourself in the other person's shoes.

Consider their feelings, motivations, and perspectives to gain a deeper understanding.

Random Acts of Kindness:

Incorporate intentional acts of kindness into your routine.

Observe how these acts affect both you and the recipients, fostering a sense of empathy.

The Five-Minute Connection:

Spend five minutes in genuine conversation with someone, focusing on understanding their emotions and experiences.

Avoid distractions and give your full attention to the interaction.

Body Language Awareness:

Pay attention to non-verbal cues in conversations, such as facial expressions and body language.

Practice interpreting and responding to these cues empathetically.

Remember, the key to empathy exercises is consistent practice. By incorporating these activities into daily life, you can develop and strengthen your empathetic abilities, creating more meaningful connections with others just like Jesus did while he was here on earth.

You are a Kingdom Connecter!

INTRODUCTION TO WEEK 6
Presence and Mindfulness

Welcome to Week 6, where the theme is "Presence and Mindfulness." This week, immerse yourself in the transformative power of being present with the words—Presence, Sustain, Nurture, Authentic, and Learn. Engage in the practice of mindfulness as you cultivate a deeper connection with the present moment and the essence of your being.

Presence:

Our exploration begins with Presence, the anchor that grounds you in the now. Like a still lake reflecting the beauty around it, allow yourself to be fully present in each moment. Presence is the gateway to a mindful existence, inviting you to savor the richness of the present and all it holds.

Sustain:

Sustain becomes the nurturing force that ensures the continuity of your mindful journey. Like a caretaker tending to a delicate garden, sustain your presence with intention and care. Embrace practices that nourish your soul and allow the essence of mindfulness to thrive and endure.

Nurture:

Nurture invites you to foster a mindful environment within and around you. Like a gardener nurturing tender shoots, cultivate a space that encourages mindfulness to flourish. Extend compassion to yourself and others, creating an atmosphere where the seeds of presence can germinate and grow.

Authentic:

Authenticity is the cornerstone of mindfulness. Like a rare gem, be true to your essence. Cultivate an authentic presence that aligns with your values and inner truth. Embrace mindfulness as a journey into your genuine self, fostering a sense of peace and harmony within.

Learn:

Learn becomes the perpetual student on your mindfulness journey. Like an explorer seeking new horizons, approach each moment with a curious spirit. Learn from the experiences the present offers, allowing each encounter to be a teacher guiding you toward a more mindful and intentional life.

As you embrace the essence of Presence and Mindfulness this week, may these words become gentle reminders to savor the beauty of the present, nurture the mindful garden within, and embrace the authenticity of your being. Let Presence, Sustain, Nurture, Authentic, and Learn be your companions on this week's journey into the transformative realms of mindfulness. Welcome to a week where each moment unfolds as a precious gift to be mindfully embraced.

Presence

"The Lord is near to all who call on him, to all who call on him in truth."

– Psalm 145:18

To embrace "Presence" is to acknowledge the promise found in Psalm 145:18—the assurance that the Lord is near to all who sincerely call upon Him. Presence, in this context, is not a distant or passive connection; it is an intimate closeness that comes from genuine and truthful communion with God. It is an invitation to experience the comforting and transformative nearness of the Divine.

Psalm 145:18 emphasizes the condition of calling on the Lord in truth. Presence is not contingent upon eloquence or rituals but on the authenticity of our connection with God. It is a reminder that in moments of prayer, reflection, and seeking, the Lord's nearness is experienced most profoundly when approached with a sincere and truthful heart.

As we reflect on the word "Presence" today, let us meditate on the comforting promise found in Psalm 145:18. May our hearts be open to the nearness of the Lord as we call upon Him in truth. In moments of communion, let us offer a prayer for sincerity and a commitment to seek His presence authentically. May our lives be characterized by a profound sense of closeness to the Divine, transforming our existence through His nearness.

Prayer:

Heavenly Father, we call upon You in truth, seeking Your nearness. May our hearts be open to the transformative presence that comes from authentic communion with You. In moments of prayer and seeking, draw near to us, and may we experience the profound closeness that Psalm 145:18 promises. Amen.

Affirmation:

"I embrace the transformative presence of the Lord. Psalm 145:18 is my assurance, and as I call upon Him in truth, I experience His nearness. My life is characterized by an intimate communion with the Divine, transforming my existence through His comforting and transformative presence."

Sustain

"Cast your burden on the Lord, and he will sustain you; he will never permit the righteous to be moved."

– Psalm 55:22

To "Sustain" is to embrace the promise embedded in Psalm 55:22—a call to cast our burdens upon the Lord with the assurance that He will sustain us. Sustenance, in this context, is not merely survival but a continuous and nurturing support that comes from entrusting our cares to God. It is an invitation to experience the unyielding strength and reliability of the Divine.

Psalm 55:22 assures that as we cast our burdens upon the Lord, He will not merely carry them, but He will actively sustain us. Sustenance in the hands of God involves a constant provision of strength, comfort, and resilience. It is a promise that extends beyond momentary relief, ensuring that the righteous, those who trust in Him, will not be moved from their foundation.

As we reflect on the word "Sustain" today, let us meditate on the comforting promise found in Psalm 55:22. May our hearts be open to casting our burdens upon the Lord, knowing that His sustenance goes beyond mere assistance. In moments of surrender, let us offer a prayer for trust and a commitment to rely on His sustaining grace. May our lives be characterized by the unshakable foundation that comes from entrusting our burdens to the Lord.

Prayer:

Merciful God, I cast my burdens upon You, knowing that You will sustain me. May my heart be open to Your continuous support and nurturing strength. In moments of surrender, help me to trust in

Your sustaining grace. May my life be characterized by the unyielding foundation that comes from entrusting my cares to You. Amen.

Affirmation:

"I cast my burdens upon the Lord, trusting in His sustaining grace. Psalm 55:22 is my assurance, and as I surrender to His continuous support, my life is characterized by unshakable resilience. I am sustained by the Divine, and in Him, I find strength and comfort."

Nurture

"Rather, speaking the truth in love, we are to grow up in every way into him who is the head, into Christ."

– Ephesians 4:15

To "Nurture" is to embody the guidance found in Ephesians 4:15—a directive to speak the truth in love, fostering a growth that aligns with Christ, the ultimate example. Nurturing, in this context, is not merely providing care but actively participating in the spiritual and personal development of oneself and others. It is an invitation to cultivate an environment where truth is spoken with love, promoting growth in every dimension.

Ephesians 4:15 underscores the transformative power of speaking truth in love. Nurturing involves not only the communication of truth but doing so in a manner that reflects Christ's love. It is a call to create a space where individuals can grow spiritually, emotionally, and mentally, aligning themselves with the example set by Christ, who is the head of this transformative journey.

As we reflect on the word "Nurture" today, let us meditate on the guidance found in Ephesians 4:15. May our hearts be open to nurturing an environment where truth is spoken in love, fostering growth in every dimension. In moments of communication and interaction, let us offer a prayer for wisdom and a commitment to nurture ourselves and others in a manner that aligns with Christ's example. May our lives be characterized by a nurturing spirit that promotes transformative growth.

Prayer:

Loving Father, guide me in the spirit of nurturing as outlined in Ephesians 4:15. May my words be a reflection of truth spoken in love, fostering growth in every dimension. In moments of inter-action, help me to create an environment that aligns with Christ's example, where individuals can grow into Him who is the head. Amen.

Affirmation:

"I embrace the spirit of nurturing in my interactions. Ephesians 4:15 guides me to speak the truth in love, fostering growth in every dimension. My life is characterized by a nurturing spirit that reflects Christ's example, and in this environment, I and others grow into Him who is the head."

Authentic

"But the Lord said to Samuel, 'Do not look on his appearance or on the height of his stature, because I have rejected him. For the Lord sees not as man sees: man looks on the outward appearance, but the Lord looks on the heart.'"

– 1 Samuel 16:7

To be "Authentic" is to heed the wisdom found in 1 Samuel 16:7—a reminder that the Lord values the authenticity of the heart over external appearances. Authenticity, in this context, is not about superficial impressions but a genuine reflection of the inner character. It is an invitation to live in alignment with the values that God sees and appreciates, transcending societal expectations.

1 Samuel 16:7 challenges the notion that external appearances define worth. Authentic living involves embracing the truth that the Lord sees beyond the surface, discerning the authenticity of the heart. It is a call to cultivate a character that reflects the values and principles that God cherishes, acknowledging that true worth is found in authenticity, not in conformity to societal standards.

As we reflect on the word "Authentic" today, let us meditate on the guidance found in 1 Samuel 16:7. May our hearts be open to living authentically, valuing inner character over external appearances. In moments of self-reflection and interaction with others, let us offer a prayer for authenticity and a commitment to align our lives with the values that the Lord cherishes. May our lives be characterized by the genuine and authentic expression of the heart.

Prayer:

Heavenly Father, guide me in the path of authenticity, as emphasized in 1 Samuel 16:7. May my heart be genuine, reflecting the values You cherish. In moments of self-reflection and interaction, help me prioritize authenticity over external appearances. May my life be characterized by a true and authentic expression of the heart. Amen.

Affirmation:

"I embrace the call to authenticity in my life. 1 Samuel 16:7 guides me to value the genuine nature of the heart. My worth is found in authenticity, and I live in alignment with the values that the Lord cherishes. I am authentically and genuinely me."

Learn

"Give instruction to a wise man, and he will be still wiser; teach a righteous man, and he will increase in learning."

– Proverbs 9:9

To "Learn" is to embrace the wisdom found in Proverbs 9:9—a recognition that wisdom and righteousness are foundations for continuous learning and growth. Learning, in this context, is not a one-time event but a lifelong journey fueled by the pursuit of wisdom and righteousness. It is an invitation to cultivate a mindset that values instruction and sees every opportunity as a chance to expand one's knowledge.

Proverbs 9:9 acknowledges the receptivity of wisdom and righteousness to instruction. Learning becomes a collaborative effort between the wise, the righteous, and the teachers. It is a dynamic process where the wise become wiser, and the righteous increase in learning through the guidance and instruction they receive. It underscores the humility and openness required for continuous growth.

As we reflect on the word "Learn" today, let us meditate on the guidance found in Proverbs 9:9. May our hearts be open to the lifelong journey of learning, grounded in wisdom and righteousness. In moments of instruction and teaching, let us offer a prayer for humility and a commitment to continuous growth. May our lives be characterized by a spirit of learning, where wisdom and righteousness guide our journey.

Prayer:

Gracious God, I open my heart to the journey of learning, as encouraged in Proverbs 9:9. May wisdom and righteousness be my foundation, and in moments of instruction, grant me humility and receptivity. Teach me, guide me, and help me to increase in learning throughout my life. Amen.

Affirmation:

"I embrace the lifelong journey of learning. Proverbs 9:9 is my guide, and with wisdom and righteousness as my foundation, I am open to instruction and teaching. I am a continual learner, growing wiser and increasing in knowledge throughout my life."

REFLECTION

<u>Presence and Mindfulness Word Search</u>

N	Y	W	H	H	R	B	S	H	C	L	E	U	P	X
L	V	B	E	E	P	P	Q	K	W	A	Y	Q	E	J
J	E	P	A	I	I	T	R	K	N	B	S	K	Q	G
U	X	K	J	U	O	T	E	E	F	L	L	A	Y	R
L	O	A	K	L	T	L	L	W	S	S	J	E	E	L
H	N	G	Z	C	R	H	R	G	D	E	U	K	F	E
K	D	S	T	T	U	J	E	L	H	J	N	S	X	A
R	T	B	F	Y	Z	F	G	N	L	Y	S	C	T	R
S	L	N	U	R	T	U	R	E	T	V	R	U	E	N
H	U	N	O	F	G	D	C	R	T	I	R	U	S	S
P	H	S	H	J	H	I	Z	B	R	X	C	Z	Y	P
E	O	M	T	O	H	I	F	X	B	Z	O	B	O	W
J	V	C	A	A	K	J	Y	Z	L	D	Q	J	L	F
P	D	A	S	L	I	L	F	M	I	R	O	C	C	U
I	T	B	H	H	G	N	U	W	M	I	U	A	Y	M

<u>WORDS:</u>

AUTHENTIC PRESENCE SUSTAIN NURTURE LEARN

INTRODUCTION TO WEEK 7

Reflection

Enter Week 7, a week dedicated to "Reflection." This transformative theme encourages you to contemplate the radiance within, manifest your aspirations, elevate your perspective, unleash your potential, and focus on the essence of your journey. Let the words—Radiant, Manifest, Elevate, Unleash, and Focus—guide you in this profound week of self-discovery and reflection.

Radiant:

Our journey begins with Radiant, a celebration of the inner light that resides within you. Like the sun casting its warm glow, recognize and embrace the radiance of your unique self. Allow this word to illuminate your path and inspire a deeper connection with the brilliance that emanates from your core.

Manifest:

Manifest is the creative force that transforms thoughts into reality. Like an artist bringing a vision to life, explore the power of manifestation in your journey. Reflect on your desires, aspirations, and the tangible steps needed to bring them into existence, allowing your dreams to manifest with purpose.

Elevate:

Elevate encourages you to rise above challenges and elevate your perspective. Like a bird soaring in the sky, reflect on ways to lift yourself beyond limitations. Cultivate a mindset that transcends obstacles, allowing you to view your journey from a higher vantage point and discover new horizons.

Unleash:

Unleash is the call to release your untapped potential. Like a river surging through its course, reflect on the barriers that may be holding you back. Allow this week to be a time of introspection, identifying and unleashing the dormant strengths and capabilities within you.

Focus:

Focus becomes the lens through which you direct your energy and attention. Like a laser sharpening its beam, reflect on what truly matters in your life. Through mindful contemplation, learn to focus on the essentials, enabling you to navigate your journey with clarity and purpose.

As you immerse yourself in the reflective theme of Week 7, may these words guide you in exploring the radiance of your being, manifesting your dreams, elevating your perspective, unleashing your potential, and focusing on the meaningful aspects of your journey. Welcome to a week where deep reflection becomes a transformative journey into the essence of your radiant and purposeful existence.

Radiant

"Those who look to him are radiant, and their faces shall never be ashamed."

– Psalm 34:5

To be "Radiant" is to embody the promise found in Psalm 34:5—a declaration that those who look to the Lord shine with a radiance that shields them from shame. Radiance, in this context, is not a fleeting glow but a perpetual light that emanates from a deep connection with God. It is an invitation to fix our gaze upon the Divine, allowing His light to illuminate and transform our countenance.

Psalm 34:5 paints a vivid picture of the transformative power of looking to the Lord. Radiance is a reflection of the inner light that comes from a trusting and devoted heart. It is a promise that as we turn our attention to God, our faces will radiate with a luminosity that dispels shame. This radiance becomes a testimony to the transformative and uplifting influence of divine connection.

As we reflect on the word "Radiant" today, let us meditate on the promise found in Psalm 34:5. May our hearts be open to the transformative power of looking to the Lord, allowing His light to radiate through us. In moments of connection with the Divine, let us offer a prayer for a radiant countenance and a commitment to turn our gaze to the source of eternal light. May our lives be characterized by a perpetual radiance that shields us from shame.

Prayer:

Heavenly Father, I fix my gaze upon You, seeking the radiance promised in Psalm 34:5. May Your light illuminate my countenance, dispelling shame and transforming me from within. In moments of connection with You, grant me a radiant spirit that testifies to the transformative power of divine communion. Amen.

Affirmation:

"I am radiant as I look to the Lord. Psalm 34:5 is my assurance, and as His light illuminates my heart, my face shines with a perpetual radiance. I am shielded from shame, and my life testifies to the transformative power of divine connection."

Manifest

"For nothing is hidden that will not be made manifest, nor is anything secret that will not be known and come to light."

– Luke 8:17

To "Manifest" is to embrace the truth found in Luke 8:17—a recognition that all that is hidden will eventually be revealed and brought into the light. Manifestation, in this context, is not just about disclosure but a divine unfolding where secrets are unveiled. It is an invitation to live with transparency, acknowledging that ultimate revelation belongs to the divine order.

Luke 8:17 speaks to the inevitability of manifestation. Nothing remains concealed from the divine gaze, and in due time, all secrets are known and brought to light. Manifestation, in this divine context, is not a cause for fear but an opportunity for truth and transformation. It is a call to live authentically, knowing that the divine light exposes all hidden things.

As we reflect on the word "Manifest" today, let us meditate on the truth found in Luke 8:17. May our hearts be open to living transparently, embracing the divine order where hidden things are made manifest. In moments of self-reflection and honesty, let us offer a prayer for authenticity and a commitment to a life that aligns with the divine light. May our lives be characterized by a spirit of manifestation, where truth prevails and authenticity shines.

Prayer:

Divine Creator, I surrender to the truth that nothing is hidden from Your sight, as mentioned in Luke 8:17. May my heart be open to living authentically, embracing the divine order where hidden things are made manifest. In moments of self-reflection, grant me the courage to align my life with the light of Your truth. Amen.

Affirmation:

"I embrace the divine order of manifestation. Luke 8:17 is my guide, and as I live authentically, all hidden things are brought into the light. I welcome the transformative power of truth, and my life is characterized by transparency and authenticity."

Elevate

"Humble yourselves before the Lord, and he will exalt you."

– James 4:10

To "Elevate" is to heed the wisdom found in James 4:10—a reminder that true exaltation comes from humble submission before the Lord. Elevation, in this context, is not achieved through self-promotion or worldly measures but through a genuine humility that acknowledges our dependence on God. It is an invitation to lower ourselves in His presence, trusting that He, in His divine wisdom, will lift us up.

James 4:10 emphasizes the divine principle of exaltation through humility. Elevation in the eyes of the Lord is a response to genuine humility, where we acknowledge our need for His guidance and surrender our pride. It is not about seeking recognition from the world but finding favor in the eyes of God, who exalts those with humble and contrite hearts.

As we reflect on the word "Elevate" today, let us meditate on the wisdom found in James 4:10. May our hearts be open to humbling ourselves before the Lord, trusting in His promise of exaltation. In moments of surrender and humility, let us offer a prayer for guidance and a commitment to a life that seeks elevation in the divine eyes. May our lives be characterized by a spirit of humility that leads to true and lasting exaltation.

Prayer:

Heavenly Father, I humbly submit myself before You, trusting in the promise of exaltation found in James 4:10. May my heart be genuinely humble, acknowledging my dependence on You. In moments of surrender, guide me, and may my life be characterized by true elevation in Your eyes. Amen.

Affirmation:

"I embrace the divine principle of elevation through humility. James 4:10 is my guide, and as I humble myself before the Lord, He exalts me in His wisdom. My life is characterized by genuine humility, and I find true exaltation in His presence."

Unleash

"But you, O Lord, are a shield about me, my glory, and the lifter of my head."

– Psalm 3:3

To "Unleash" is to revel in the assurance found in Psalm 3:3—a recognition that the Lord is not only a protective shield but also the source of glory and the lifter of our heads. Unleashing, in this context, is not just about breaking free from constraints but about embracing the fullness of God's role in our lives. It is an invitation to release our burdens, knowing that the Lord surrounds us, uplifts our spirits, and bestows glory upon us.

Psalm 3:3 portrays the multifaceted role of the Lord. He is not merely a shield offering protection; He is the source of our glory and the lifter of our heads in times of distress. Unleashing becomes an act of trust, allowing the Lord to take control, defend us, and raise us up. It is a recognition that our true strength and glory come from being in His presence.

As we reflect on the word "Unleash" today, let us meditate on the assurance found in Psalm 3:3. May our hearts be open to unleashing our burdens before the Lord, acknowledging Him as our shield, glory, and the lifter of our heads. In moments of surrender and trust, let us offer a prayer for divine intervention and a commitment to a life that unleashes the fullness of God's role in our journey. May our lives be characterized by the freedom that comes from trusting in the Lord's protection, glory, and uplifting grace.

Prayer:

O Lord, I unleash my burdens before You, trusting in Your role as my shield, glory, and the lifter of my head, as described in Psalm

3:3. May my heart be open to divine intervention, and in moments of surrender, be my shield, source of glory, and the lifter of my head. Amen.

Affirmation:

"I unleash my burdens before the Lord, trusting in His role as my shield, glory, and the lifter of my head. Psalm 3:3 is my assurance, and in surrender, I find freedom and fullness in His protective, glorious, and uplifting presence."

Focus

> "Let your eyes look directly forward, and your gaze be straight before you."
>
> *– Proverbs 4:25*

To "Focus" is to embrace the wisdom found in Proverbs 4:25—a directive to keep our eyes fixed on the path ahead. Focus, in this context, is not merely about concentration but about deliberate alignment with a purposeful direction. It is an invitation to set our gaze straight before us, avoiding distractions, and staying committed to the journey that lies ahead.

Proverbs 4:25 encourages a forward-looking perspective. Focus involves more than avoiding peripheral distractions; it is about maintaining a steadfast commitment to our goals and purposes. It is a call to resist the pull of diversions and keep our eyes fixed on the path, ensuring that our journey is guided by purpose and intentionality.

As we reflect on the word "Focus" today, let us meditate on the guidance found in Proverbs 4:25. May our hearts be open to the discipline of maintaining a forward-looking gaze. In moments of potential distraction and wavering commitment, let us offer a prayer for steadfastness and a commitment to a life that is characterized by intentional focus on the path ahead. May our journey be purposeful, guided by unwavering dedication.

Prayer:

Heavenly Father, guide me in the discipline of focus, as encouraged in Proverbs 4:25. May my eyes look directly forward, and my gaze be straight before me. In moments of distraction and uncertainty, grant me steadfastness and commitment to the purposeful journey ahead. Amen.

Affirmation:

"I embrace the discipline of focus in my journey. Proverbs 4:25 is my guide, and with eyes looking directly forward and a gaze straight before me, my life is characterized by intentional focus on the path ahead. I am committed, purposeful, and unwavering in my dedication."

REFLECTION

<u>Intentional Practice Guide Action Plan</u>

1. Reflect on Radiance and Aspirations:
   - Recall moments of radiance in your life.
   - Define specific goals you want to manifest in personal growth, relationships, career, or well-being.

2. Elevate Your Awareness:
   - Identify areas needing heightened awareness.
   - Plan steps to elevate consciousness.

3. Unleash Your Potential:
   - Identify and plan to unleash your potential in one area where you've held back.

4. Focus and Prioritize:
   - Choose a radiant living goal that aligns with your aspirations.
   - Detail specific actions for the coming weeks to manifest, elevate, and unleash.

5. Develop an Action Plan:
   - Create a concrete, daily-action plan with clear, achievable steps.
   - Break down tasks related to manifesting, elevating awareness, and unleashing potential.

This comprehensive action plan is your roadmap for the radiant living journey. Regularly revisit your reflections and action plans to stay aligned with your goals, allowing the radiant energy within you to guide your personal development and illuminate the path to a fulfilling life.

Continue to shine bright!

Serenity and Renewal

Welcome to the culminating week, Week 8, where the theme is "Serenity and Renewal." This transformative week invites you to radiate the peace within, embrace serenity, engage in the renewing power of self-reflection, empower your intentions, and align your journey with a sense of purpose. Let the words—Radiate, Serenity, Renew, Empower/Intent, and Align—guide you in this final stage of your enriching journey.

Radiate:

Our exploration begins with Radiate, an invitation to share the inner peace that resides within you. Like a gentle breeze spreading tranquility, reflect on how you can radiate serenity to those around you. Let your inner calm be a source of comfort and inspiration for others on their journeys.

Serenity:

Serenity becomes the serene lake of tranquility that mirrors your inner peace. Like a still pond reflecting the beauty of the surrounding landscape, delve into the essence of serenity within yourself. Cultivate moments of calm reflection and inner stillness, allowing serenity to be a guiding force.

Renew:

Renew is the refreshing stream that revitalizes your spirit. Like a clear stream flowing through a forest, reflect on the renewing power of self-reflection and intentional rejuvenation. Consider the practices that bring renewal to your mind, body, and soul, ensuring a continuous and purposeful journey.

Empower/Intent:

Empower or Intent is the beacon guiding your actions with purpose. Like a compass pointing north, reflect on the intentions that empower your journey. Consider the alignment between your aspirations and your actions, empowering each step with clear intent and unwavering purpose.

Align:

Align becomes the cosmic dance, bringing your journey into harmonious unity. Like celestial bodies aligning in the night sky, reflect on the alignment of your journey with your deeper purpose. Consider how each step aligns with your values, creating a trajectory that resonates with authenticity and fulfillment.

As you conclude this transformative journey of "Serenity and Renewal" in Week 8, may these words guide you in radiating peace, embracing serenity, renewing your spirit, empowering your intentions, and aligning your journey with a sense of purpose. Welcome to a week where serenity and renewal become the gentle winds that carry you into the next chapter of your unlimited life.

Radiate

"Arise, shine, for your light has come, and the glory of the Lord has risen upon you."

– Isaiah 60:1

To "Radiate" is to respond to the divine call in Isaiah 60:1—an invitation to arise and shine, for the light of the Lord has dawned upon us. Radiance, in this context, is not a passive state but an active response to the illumination of God's glory. It is an acknowledgment that the divine light within us is meant to shine forth, dispelling darkness and revealing the splendor of His presence.

Isaiah 60:1 paints a picture of a transformative moment. Radiating involves recognizing that the light of the Lord has come, and as a result, we are called to shine. It is not a self-generated brilliance but a reflection of the glory that has risen upon us. It is a call to embrace the divine light within and allow it to radiate outward, illuminating our lives and the lives of those around us.

As we reflect on the word "Radiate" today, let us meditate on the call found in Isaiah 60:1. May our hearts be open to arising and shining, allowing the light of the Lord to radiate within us. In moments of divine illumination, let us offer a prayer for boldness and a commitment to a life that is characterized by radiance, revealing the glory of the Lord to the world.

Prayer:

Gracious Lord, I respond to Your call to arise and shine, for Your light has come. May the glory of the Lord rise upon me, and in moments of divine illumination, grant me the boldness to radiate Your light. May my life be characterized by a radiance that reveals Your splendor to the world. Amen.

Affirmation:

"I arise and shine, for the light of the Lord has come. Isaiah 60:1 is my call, and as His glory rises upon me, my life is characterized by a radiant illumination. I boldly radiate His light, revealing the splendor of His presence to the world."

Serenity

"And the peace of God, which surpasses all understanding, will guard your hearts and your minds in Christ Jesus."

– Philippians 4:7

The concept of serenity holds profound significance. Serenity is not merely the absence of chaos but the presence of inner peace, a tranquil state of mind amidst life's storms. It's the calm assurance that comes from surrendering to the divine, trusting in the greater plan unfolding before us. Just as a serene lake reflects the beauty of the sky above, our inner serenity reflects the peace of God dwelling within us, transcending all understanding.

In Philippians 4:7, we find reassurance in the promise of God's peace, a peace that surpasses human comprehension and guards our hearts and minds in Christ Jesus. This scripture reminds us that amidst life's uncertainties and challenges, we can find refuge in the unshakable peace that comes from our relationship with God. It's a peace that envelops us like a comforting embrace, guiding us through life's journey with unwavering faith and serenity.

Prayer:

Heavenly Father, in the midst of life's turbulence, we seek the serenity that only You can provide. May Your peace, which surpasses all understanding, guard our hearts and minds in Christ Jesus. Grant us the strength to surrender our worries and anxieties to You, trusting in Your divine plan for our lives. Fill us with Your presence, Lord, and let Your peace reign within us, anchoring us in the assurance of Your love and care. Amen.

Affirmation:

"I am enveloped in the peace of God, which surpasses all understanding. His divine presence guards my heart and mind, filling me with serenity amidst life's challenges. I trust in His plan for my life, knowing that His peace guides me through every moment with unwavering faith."

Renew

> "But they who wait for the Lord shall renew their strength; they shall mount up with wings like eagles; they shall run and not be weary; they shall walk and not faint."
>
> *– Isaiah 40:31*

To "Renew" is to embrace the promise found in Isaiah 40:31—a declaration that those who patiently wait for the Lord will experience a renewal of strength. Renewal, in this context, is not a superficial refresh but a profound rejuvenation that empowers us to soar to new heights. It is an invitation to patiently trust in the Lord, knowing that He is the source of enduring strength.

Isaiah 40:31 portrays a vivid image of the transformative power of waiting on the Lord. Renewal involves mounting up with wings like eagles, symbolizing the freedom and strength that come from divine waiting. It is a promise that as we patiently trust in the Lord, our strength will be rejuvenated to the point where weariness and fainting become distant concerns.

As we reflect on the word "Renew" today, let us meditate on the promise found in Isaiah 40:31. May our hearts be open to patiently waiting on the Lord, trusting in His promise of strength renewal. In moments of waiting and anticipation, let us offer a prayer for endurance and a commitment to a life that is characterized by a continual renewal of strength through our connection with the Lord.

Prayer:

Heavenly Father, I wait patiently for You, trusting in the promise of strength renewal found in Isaiah 40:31. May my strength be continually rejuvenated by Your divine power. In moments of waiting, grant me endurance, and may my life be characterized by a deep and enduring renewal through my connection with You. Amen.

Affirmation:

"I patiently wait for the Lord, knowing that in His time, my strength will be renewed. Isaiah 40:31 is my assurance, and as I trust in Him, I mount up with wings like eagles. My life is characterized by a continual renewal of strength, and I soar to new heights through my connection with the Lord."

Empower

> "I can do all things through him who strengthens me."
> *– Philippians 4:13 (Repeated for emphasis)*

To "Empower" is to declare the profound truth emphasized in Philippians 4:13—an affirmation that our abilities are limitless through the strength derived from Him. Empowerment, in this context, is not rooted in self-reliance but in a deep connection with the One who provides unwavering strength. It is an invitation to recognize the boundless potential that comes from relying on His empowering grace.

Philippians 4:13 serves as a beacon of inspiration. Empowerment involves acknowledging our dependence on the strength that comes from Him. It is a declaration that, through this divine connection, we can overcome challenges, exceed expectations, and accomplish all things. It is a call to tap into the limitless source of strength and empowerment that resides in our relationship with Him.

As we reflect on the word "Empower" today, let us meditate on the empowering truth found in Philippians 4:13. May our hearts be open to the realization that, through Him, we can do all things. In moments of self-doubt or challenge, let us offer a prayer for empowerment and a commitment to living a life characterized by the boundless strength that comes from our connection with Him.

Prayer:

Mighty God, I acknowledge my dependence on You for strength and empowerment as declared in Philippians 4:13. May my life be characterized by the limitless potential that comes from relying on Your empowering grace. In moments of challenge, grant me the confidence to declare, 'I can do all things through Him who strengthens me.' Amen.

Affirmation:

"I am empowered through Him who strengthens me. Philippians 4:13 is my declaration, and in His strength, my abilities are limitless. I embrace the empowering truth that, through Him, I can overcome challenges, exceed expectations, and accomplish all things."

Align

"Trust in the Lord with all your heart, and do not lean on your own understanding."

– Proverbs 3:5

To "Align" is to heed the wisdom found in Proverbs 3:5—a call to place complete trust in the Lord with unwavering faith. Alignment, in this context, is not about relying solely on human understanding but surrendering to divine wisdom and guidance. It is an invitation to synchronize our hearts with the Lord's purpose and direction, acknowledging that His understanding surpasses our own.

Proverbs 3:5 offers a transformative perspective on alignment. It calls us to trust in the Lord with every fiber of our being, releasing our reliance on limited human understanding. Alignment involves surrendering our plans, thoughts, and desires to the divine, allowing His wisdom to guide our paths. It is a call to synchronize our hearts with His, fostering a harmonious and purposeful life.

As we reflect on the word "Align" today, let us meditate on the guidance found in Proverbs 3:5. May our hearts be open to complete trust in the Lord, surrendering our understanding to His divine wisdom. In moments of decision and uncertainty, let us offer a prayer for alignment and a commitment to a life characterized by syncing our hearts with His purpose and direction.

Prayer:

Heavenly Father, I trust in You with all my heart, as Proverbs 3:5 guides me. May my understanding align with Your divine wisdom. In moments of decision, uncertainty, and planning, grant me the grace to surrender and align my heart with Your purpose. Amen.

Affirmation:

"I trust in the Lord with all my heart. Proverbs 3:5 is my guide, and as I align my understanding with His divine wisdom, my life is characterized by purposeful and harmonious alignment with His perfect plan."

REFLECTION

<u>Serenity and Renewal Word Search</u>

M	O	W	M	U	E	J	U	P	G	J	V	V	Q	S
I	S	L	E	Q	Q	Y	P	A	M	O	L	K	E	J
S	N	C	E	B	L	U	R	L	B	W	H	G	X	B
E	M	T	X	M	N	N	X	I	G	B	J	V	T	T
S	V	L	E	E	P	N	S	G	V	D	W	N	Q	V
S	Q	S	I	N	I	O	O	N	S	R	T	N	G	N
E	G	O	I	S	T	E	W	S	W	E	B	E	L	K
L	L	X	B	M	E	H	I	E	S	N	U	J	K	L
V	X	T	M	G	W	R	D	R	R	E	Y	G	R	I
O	Y	Y	E	E	F	I	E	W	N	W	S	W	C	N
A	E	K	A	E	X	R	I	N	W	D	E	A	X	K
R	A	D	I	A	T	E	K	L	I	X	J	Z	O	V
M	Y	C	Z	D	A	P	G	T	F	T	X	X	T	U
G	E	U	Q	A	F	T	L	C	S	D	Y	Z	Z	M
Y	K	L	I	V	R	G	N	C	A	J	R	J	R	T

<u>WORDS:</u>

**SERENITY RADIATE EMPOWER
ALIGN INTENT RENEW**

As we wrap up this incredible 40-day journey exploring the transformative themes of Unlimited Life, we find ourselves at the crossroads of personal development, spirituality, and mindful living. Throughout this expedition, we've delved into words of profound significance, drawing inspiration from timeless scriptures – from Clarity to Empowerment, each word a stepping stone in our pursuit of a life without limits. Now, it's time for the Reset for Transformation.

Heartfelt congratulations on completing this 40-day odyssey of self-discovery! The reset you've experienced has set the stage for a revitalized and empowered life. Take a moment now to reflect on the remarkable changes within and around you. Your commitment to daily reflection and intentional growth has paved the way for a life that knows no bounds.

Now, your call to action:

Let this transformation be the spark for ongoing change. Seize each day as an opportunity to live with purpose, radiate positivity, and align with your core values. Keep embracing mindfulness, empathy, and intentional living. Share the wisdom gained, creating a ripple effect of positive transformation in the lives of those around you.

As you move forward, carry the invaluable lessons of this devotional in your heart. Be deliberate in nurturing relationships, facing challenges with resilience, and cultivating a growth mindset. Remember, this journey is far from over; it's a continuous process of evolution and self-discovery.

Empower yourself to set new goals, explore uncharted territories, and remain aligned with your true purpose. The empathic reset you've undergone is a lifelong gift. Keep the flame of transformation alive, and may your life unfold in abundance, authenticity, and boundless joy.

Thank you for embarking on this transformative journey. May you radiate the power of transformation you've cultivated, inspiring others to embark on their paths of unlimited life. Embrace the endless possibilities that await, and continue to thrive in the abundant life you've crafted through these 40 days of intentional transformation.

Answer Key

Foundations of Growth Crossword Puzzle

Across:

  2. Growth   5. Resilience

Down:

  1. Gratitude   3. Courage   4. Balance

Transformative Power Word Search

H	E	T	R	A	N	S	F	O	R	M	D	K	P	R
P	V	P	V	K	X	U	N	Y	D	P	A	V	S	W
R	E	K	B	F	U	K	H	V	G	O	L	I	V	A
U	T	R	L	O	A	X	H	S	V	T	Y	J	J	G
A	P	R	S	X	Z	X	S	N	H	V	R	E	L	O
W	O	X	T	E	J	U	A	V	F	J	U	P	H	J
I	E	F	N	O	V	N	S	D	C	A	N	A	R	U
S	T	B	E	O	U	E	F	W	R	Q	J	A	T	M
D	P	V	B	L	O	V	R	T	E	N	V	Q	I	L
O	A	F	X	G	S	A	V	E	F	N	O	F	E	T
M	B	M	A	O	G	D	E	U	L	C	K	T	N	C
G	Q	O	E	H	Z	A	Q	D	E	P	H	J	N	H
M	W	T	J	Z	E	P	D	V	C	N	P	Z	X	F
B	B	O	P	Z	S	T	X	Z	T	B	M	W	S	Q
W	K	S	Q	T	G	S	Q	Y	Z	O	M	U	N	D

Visionary Living Crossword Puzzle

Across:

2. Abundance   3. Patience   5. Optimize

Down:

1. Integrity   4. Vision

Presence and Mindfulness Crossword Puzzle

N	Y	W	H	H	R	B	S	H	C	L	E	U	P	X
L	V	B	E	E	P	P	Q	K	W	A	Y	Q	E	J
J	E	P	A	I	I	T	R	K	N	B	S	K	Q	G
U	X	K	J	U	O	T	E	E	F	L	L	A	Y	R
L	O	A	K	L	T	L	L	W	S	S	J	E	E	L
H	N	G	Z	C	R	H	R	G	D	E	U	K	F	E
K	D	S	T	T	U	J	E	L	H	J	N	S	X	A
R	T	B	F	Y	Z	F	G	N	L	Y	S	C	T	R
S	L	N	U	R	T	U	R	E	T	V	R	U	E	N
H	U	N	O	F	G	D	C	R	T	I	R	U	S	S
P	H	S	H	J	H	I	Z	B	R	X	C	Z	Y	P
E	O	M	T	O	H	I	F	X	B	Z	O	B	O	W
J	V	C	A	A	K	J	Y	Z	L	D	Q	J	L	F
P	D	A	S	L	I	L	F	M	I	R	O	C	C	U
I	T	B	H	H	G	N	U	W	M	I	U	A	Y	M

Serenity and Renewal Crossword Puzzle

M	O	W	M	U	E	J	U	P	G	J	V	V	Q	S
I	S	L	E	Q	Q	Y	P	A	M	O	L	K	E	J
S	N	C	E	B	L	U	R	L	B	W	H	G	X	B
E	M	T	X	M	N	N	X	I	G	B	J	V	T	T
S	V	L	E	E	P	N	S	G	V	D	W	N	Q	V
S	Q	S	I	N	I	O	O	N	S	R	T	N	G	N
E	G	O	I	S	T	E	W	S	W	E	B	E	L	K
L	L	X	B	M	E	H	I	E	S	N	U	J	K	L
V	X	T	M	G	W	R	D	R	R	E	Y	G	R	I
O	Y	Y	E	E	F	I	E	W	N	W	S	W	C	N
A	E	K	A	E	X	R	I	N	W	D	E	A	X	K
R	A	D	I	A	T	E	K	L	I	X	J	Z	O	V
M	Y	C	Z	D	A	P	G	T	F	T	X	X	T	U
G	E	U	Q	A	F	T	L	C	S	D	Y	Z	Z	M
Y	K	L	I	V	R	G	N	C	A	J	R	J	R	T